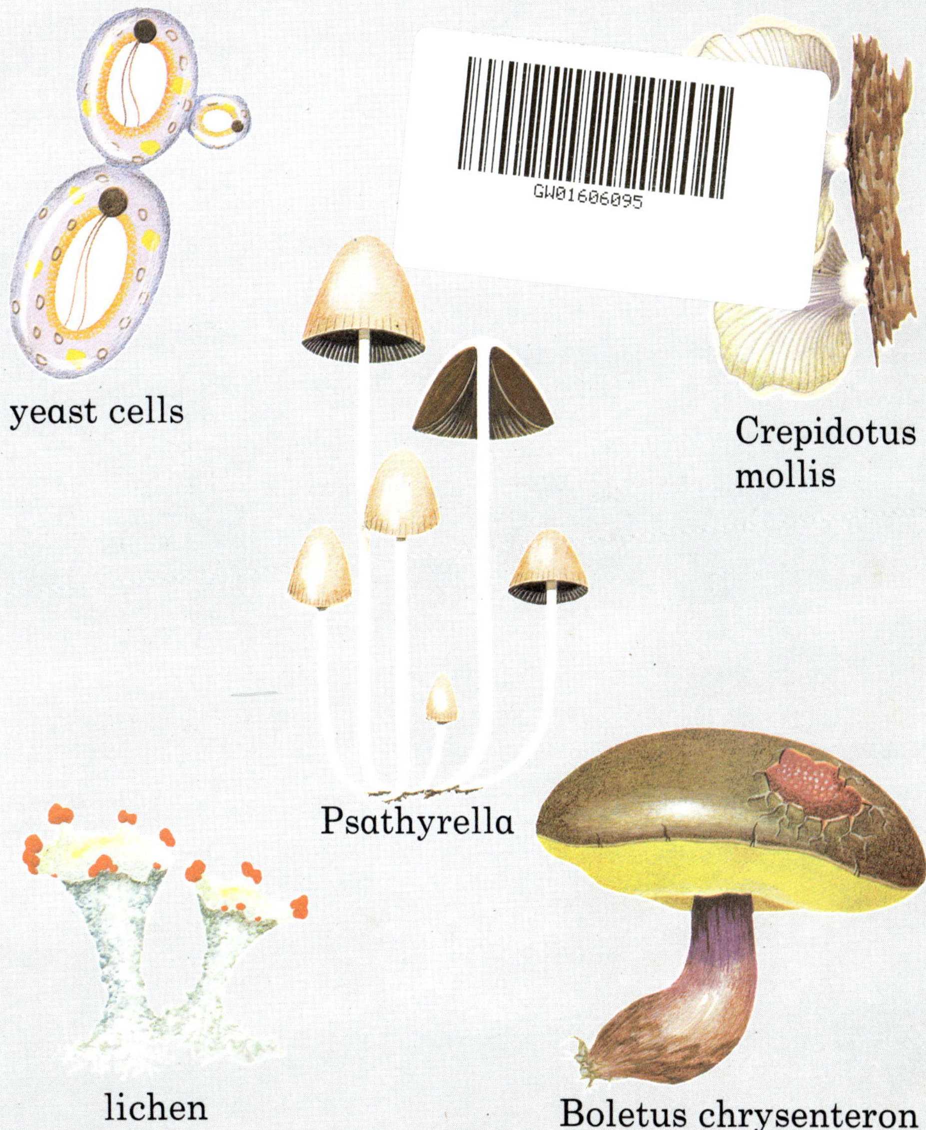
yeast cells
Crepidotus mollis
Psathyrella
lichen
Boletus chrysenteron

First Published in 1970 by
Macdonald and Company
(Publishers) Limited
St. Giles House
49-50 Poland Street
London W1

Managing Editor
Michael W. Dempsey B.A.
Chief Editor
Angela Sheehan B.A.

SBN 356 03425 9
MFL 15

Made and printed in Great Britain
by A. Wheaton & Company
Exeter Devon

MACDONALD FIRST LIBRARY

Mushrooms and Toadstools

Macdonald Educational
49-50 Poland Street
London W1

Most plants have green leaves and flowers. Mushrooms and toadstools are different. They are plants, but they do not have green leaves or flowers.
They belong to a family of plants called fungi.

If you go into the fields early on autumn mornings, you may see mushrooms growing in the grass. They look like little umbrellas. Some toadstools grow in 'fairy rings'.

Many mushrooms are good to eat. But some are poisonous. You have to be very careful not to eat poisonous fungi. Only experts know which ones you can eat.

There are many different kinds of fungi.
This is the common meadow mushroom.
The part of the mushroom that you can see has a stalk and a cap.

On the stalk there is a ragged ring of skin.
Under the cap there are 'gills'.
The gills grow out like the spokes of a bicycle wheel.

The mushroom has no roots.
Under the ground there are little white threads.
The stalk of a mushroom is made of lots and lots of these little threads.
When mushrooms first appear above the ground they look like small round buttons.
The skin on the cap stretches right around the cap to the stalk.

Green plants use sunshine to make food in their leaves.
Mushrooms cannot make their own food.
They live on dead leaves and wood in the soil.

First, a special juice is made inside the little threads in the soil.
The juice comes out of the threads into the soil.

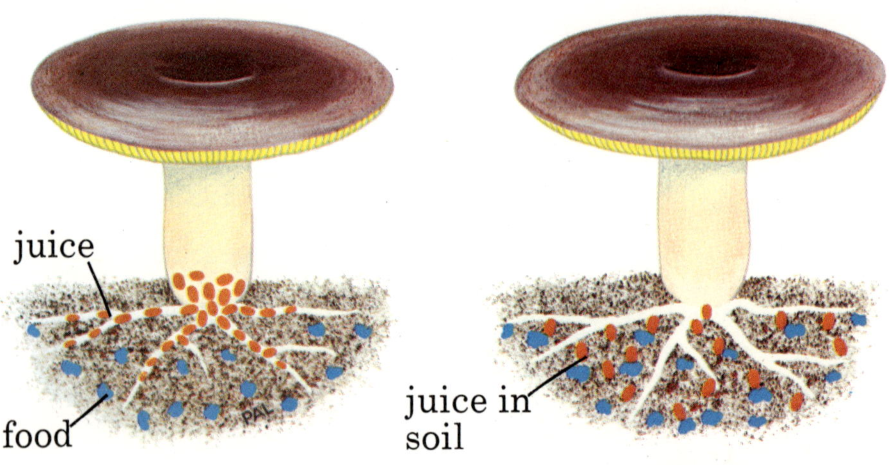

The juice dissolves the dead food, to make it easy for the mushroom to 'eat'.

The threads then take in the mixture of juice and food from the soil.

The food travels up the threads to the stalk. Then it goes up the threads in the stalk to the cap.

Some fungi grow on trees. They eat the wood of the tree, in the same way.

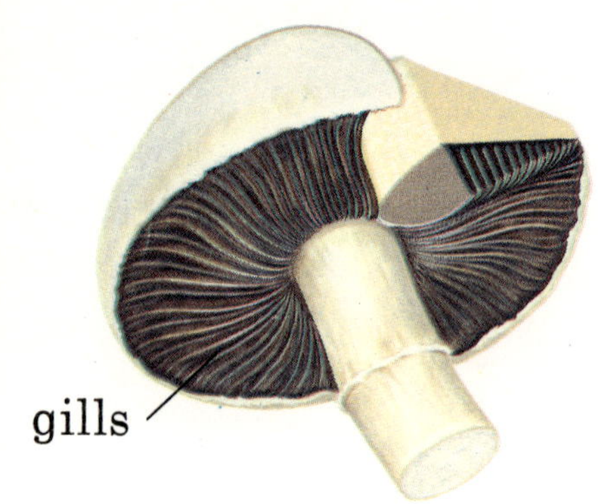

If you look underneath the cap of a mushroom, you will see its gills.
On each gill there are spores.
Spores are rather like seeds.
New mushrooms will grow from them.
The cap of the mushroom protects the spores from the rain, just like an ordinary umbrella.

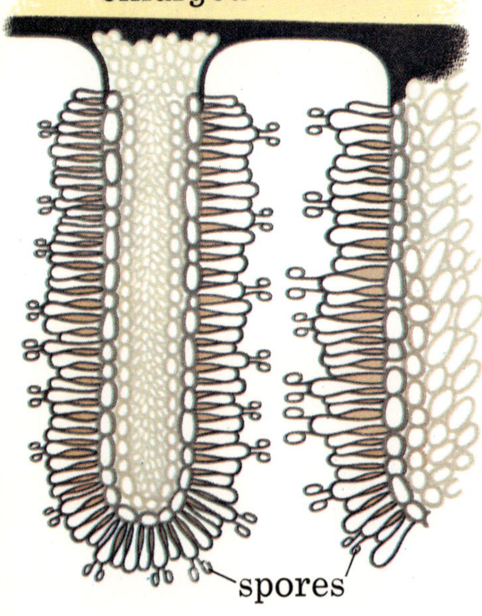

Thousands of spores hang from each gill.
This picture shows just a tiny part of one gill.

The best way to see spores is to take the stalk off a mushroom. Then put the mushroom on a piece of blotting paper.

Leave the mushroom on the paper overnight. When you pick up the mushroom in the morning, you will see the pattern of the gills on the paper.

The pattern is made from millions of spores. Just think how small a single spore must be!

pattern of spores

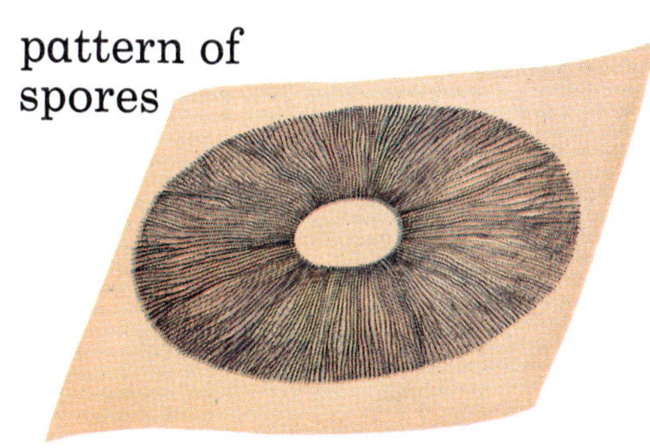

spore puts out thread

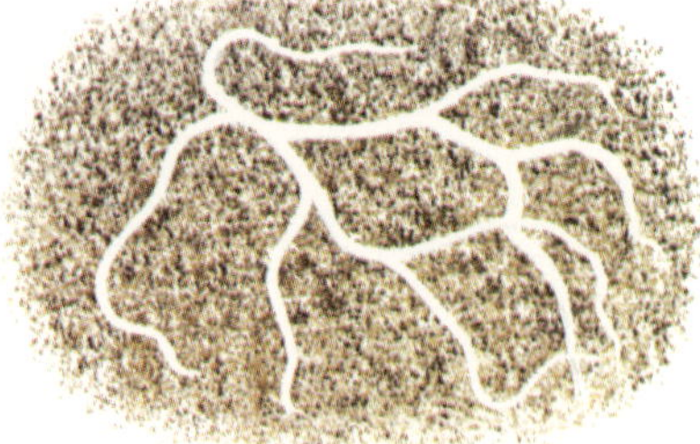

threads spread

small button grows

Mushrooms grow very fast.
The spores are blown by the wind.
If they land where there is plenty of food, they start to grow.
They do not grow roots and shoots like green plants.

The spore puts out small threads.
These threads grow branches.
Some of the branches join together to make a small 'button', no bigger than the head of a pin.

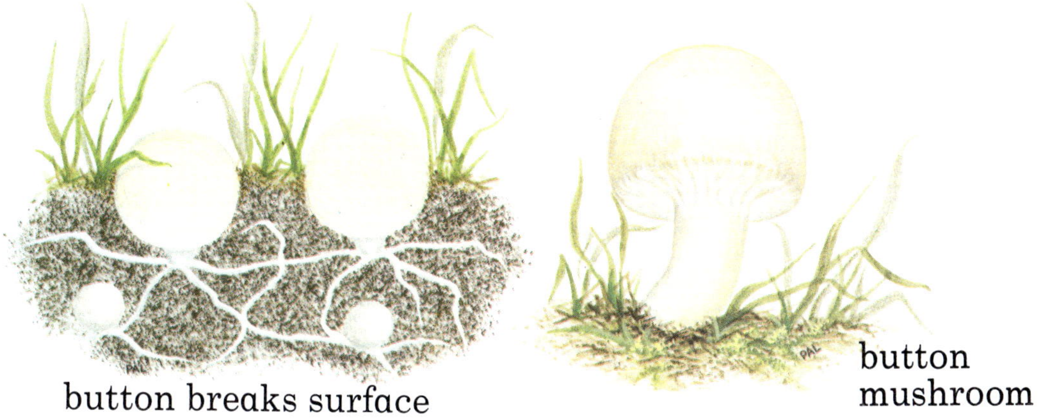

button breaks surface

button mushroom

The little button takes in food and grows until it breaks through the surface.
It grows bigger and bigger.
Soon it is too big for its skin.
The skin breaks and the little button cap spreads out, like an umbrella.
A ragged ring of skin is left on the stalk.

skin breaks

mushroom with ripe spores

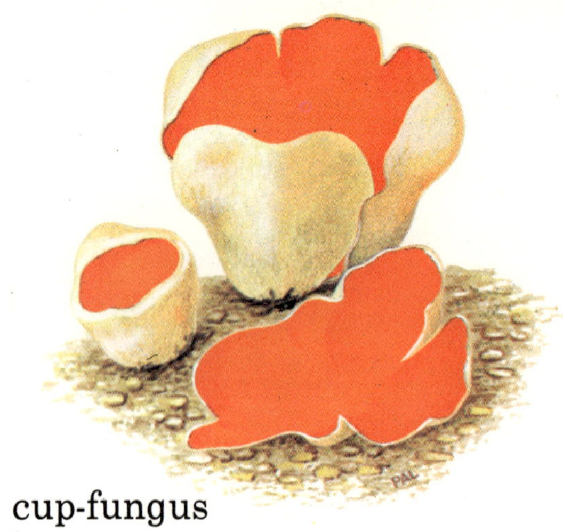

There are many different kinds of fungi.
Moulds are fungi.
Moulds usually grow on things that are rotting.
They often grow on food that is damp, or that has been left, to go 'bad'.
Pin-mould grows on cheese and bread.

The cup-fungus is another kind of fungus.
The spores grow inside the cup.

Bracket-fungi live on trees.
They cause a lot of damage to the wood.
Often there are many bracket-fungi growing, like shelves, on the branch of a tree.
Each year a new 'shelf' grows.
Some bracket-fungi are as big as pillows.

Yellow-stalk toadstools are very small.
They have thin, slimy stalks.

bracket-fungus

yellow-stalk toadstools

Fungi grow in all sorts of places.
These fungi grow on the ground.
The morel has a hollow stalk.

The death-cap toadstool is very poisonous.
It has a ring of skin round the top of its stalk and a 'cup' at the bottom.
When it first comes up, the toadstool has a pointed white cap, but this soon flattens and goes a darker colour.

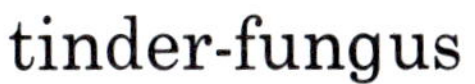

Many fungi grow on trees.

The tinder fungus grows on trees that have been injured.
If it is allowed to stay on the tree it destroys the wood completely.

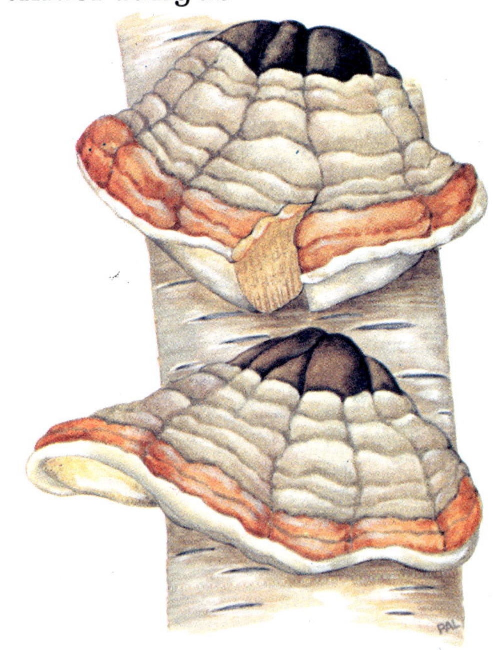

Some fungi that grow on trees have stalks.
This pretty yellow fungus grows in clumps on trees.
It is called sulphur-tuft.

sulphur-tuft

Many mushrooms and toadstools grow in woods. Different kinds grow in different kinds of woods.

In pine or birch woods, you may see the prettiest toadstool of all.
It is the fly agaric.
It has a red cap and white spots.
The white spots are patches of skin which stick to the cap.

The fly agaric looks very pretty, but it is very dangerous to eat.

fly agaric

We can see fungi on trees
and on the ground.
But some fungi, such as
truffles, grow under the
ground.
Truffles are very good to
eat but very hard to find.
Pigs love truffles and can
smell where they are.
Some farmers train pigs
to find truffles for them.

Some fungi grow on mountains and on open land.
They grow in high places where the soil is too poor for trees to grow.
Some of them like wet, boggy ground.

The horsehair toadstool grows from the stalks of other plants.
It has a long, stiff stalk like a horse's hair.

Some fungi always grow amongst the leaves of a plant called sphagnum.

Many mushrooms grow in meadows.

The shaggy ink-cap is very strange.
When it is ripe its cap curls back.
As it curls it dissolves into a black liquid.
The drips fall to the ground until the cap has disappeared completely.

Giant puff-balls often grow in meadows.
Some are as big as footballs.
Some mushrooms grow in 'fairy rings'.
Fairy rings are made because the threads
under the soil grow outwards in a circle.
Each year the circle grows bigger.
The threads in the middle of the circle die.

field mushroom

boletus (cep) mushroom

Some mushrooms are very good to eat. You can buy field mushrooms in shops. But these mushrooms are not picked from fields. They are specially grown by farmers. They are kept warm and damp, and out of the sun. The sun would shrivel them up.

The boletus (cep) fungus has tubes instead of gills beneath its cap. The tubes are taken off before it is cooked.

Chanterelles look like umbrellas that have been turned inside out.
They smell like apricots and taste very good indeed.

chanterelle

The beef-steak fungus is very big.
It grows mostly on oak trees.
Its flesh looks and feels like red meat.
But it does not taste as good.

beef-steak fungus

penicillium mould

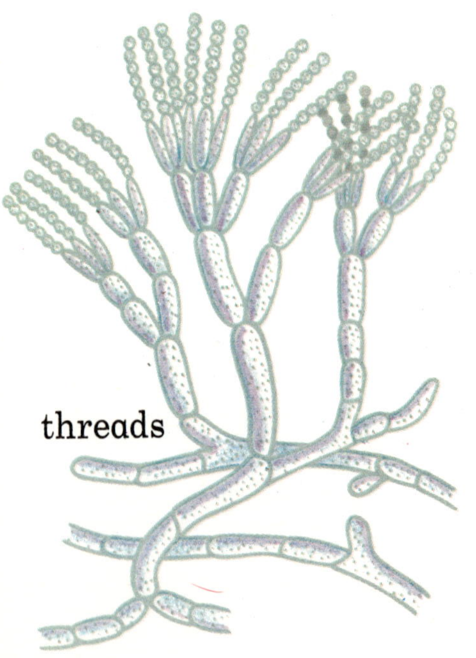

Some fungi are very useful.
A mould that sometimes grows on bread is called penicillium.
The fluffy mould is made of thousands of tiny threads like these.
They are far too small to be seen without a microscope.

A scientist, called Alexander Fleming, discovered that this mould could kill germs. Now the penicillium mould is specially 'grown' and made into a drug called penicillin. Penicillin is used to cure many diseases, from sore throats to scarlet fever. Many people would have died without penicillin.

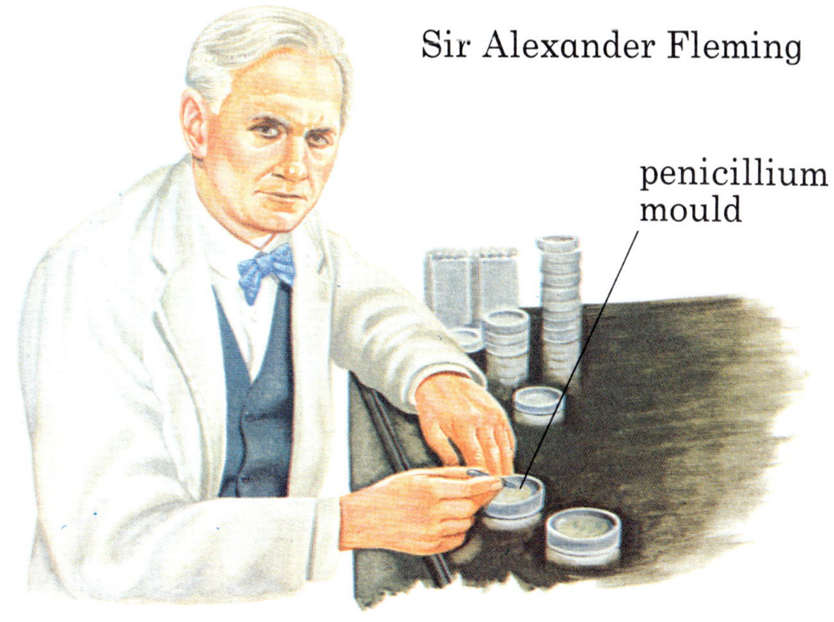

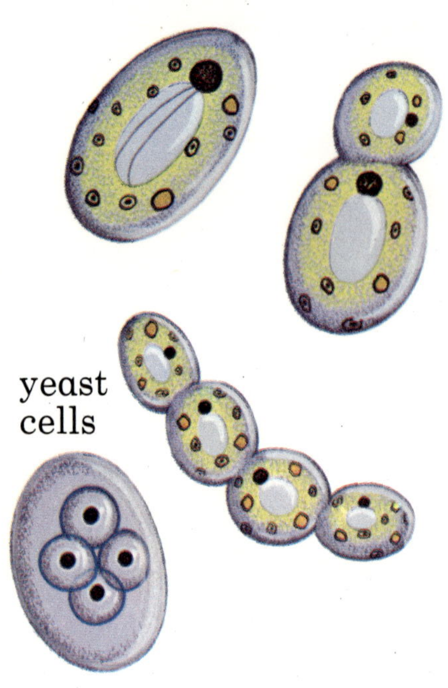

Another useful fungus is called yeast.
Yeast is used to make bread and to make beer.
The picture shows tiny yeast cells.
Yeast cells feed on sugar and on starch.
As they feed, they give off a gas called carbon dioxide.

Bakers make dough for bread from flour, sugar, milk and water.
There is a lot of starch in flour.
If the dough were cooked it would be flat and hard.
But the baker adds yeast to the dough.
The yeast feeds on the sugar and starch, and gives off bubbles of carbon dioxide.
These bubbles are trapped in the dough and make it rise.
When it is cooked, the bread is soft and light.

dry-rot fungus

Many fungi do a great deal of damage.
Dry-rot fungus attacks wood and furniture in houses.
The fungus eats away the wood.
Dry-rot can make wooden floors and walls crumble.
The fungus grows on damp wood and spreads very quickly.

Fungi often cause diseases in plants. Ergot is a disease in rye caused by a fungus. People who eat bread made from the diseased rye become very ill.

Another fungus causes potato blight. The fungus attacks the leaves of the plant and the potatoes under the soil begin to rot. Once, in Ireland, this blight ruined all the potato crops and many people starved.

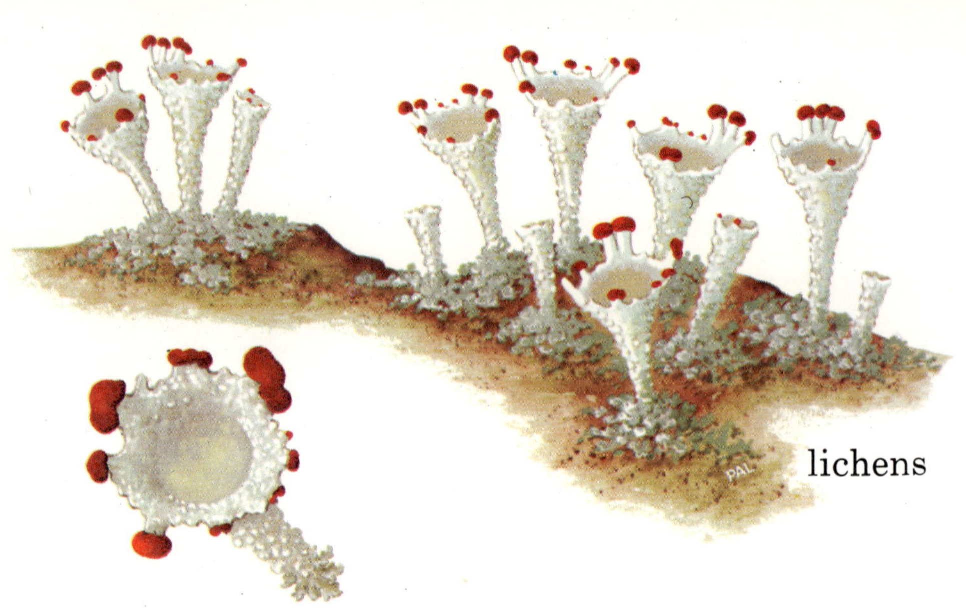

Lichens are strange plants.
They are not one plant but two.
Part of the lichen is a fungus and part of it is a plant called an alga.
The alga and the fungus live together and help each other to live.

Because these plants help each other, lichens can grow where normal fungi cannot grow.

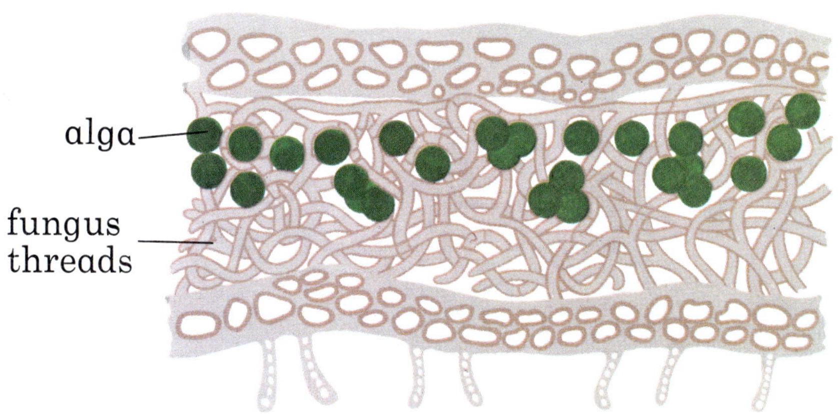

This is the inside of a lichen.
You can see the small green algae amongst the threads of the fungus.

Lichens grow on bare rocks where there is no food for the fungus.
The algae can make food from the sunlight and from the water which the fungus stores.
So the algae feed the fungus.

Index

Alga, 30, 31

Beef-steak fungus, 23
Bracket-fungus, 13
Boletus, 22

Chanterelle, 23
Cup-fungus, 12

Death-cap toadstool, 14
Dry-rot fungus, 28

Ergot, 29

Fairy ring, 2, 3, 21
Field mushroom, 22
Fly agaric, 16

Gills, 4, 5, 8

Horsehair toadstool, 19

Lichen, 30, 31

Morel, 14

Penicillin, 24, 25
Pin-mould, 12

Plant diseases, 29
Potato blight, 29
Puff-ball, 21

Shaggy ink-cap, 20, 21
Spores, 8, 9
Sulphur-tuft, 15

Tinder-fungus, 15
Truffle, 17

Yeast, 26, 27
Yellow-stalk, 13

Helvella crispa
Marasmius ramealis
inside of shaggy cap.
Coprinus comatus (shaggy cap)
Russula emetica
Peziza aurantia (orange peel)